Switzerland Travel Guide

2023-2024

A Travel Guide to Coastal Charms, Hidden Gems, and Family-Friendly Escapes.

Charles M. Dotson

All rights reserved.

No part of this publication may be reproduced, distributed, or transmitted in any form or by any means, including photocopying, recording, or other electronic or mechanical methods, without the prior written permission of the publisher, except in the case of brief quotations embodied in critical reviews and certain other noncommercial uses permitted by copyright law.

Copyright ©Charles M. Dotson, 2023.

Table Of Contents

Introduction — 4
   1. Getting to Know Switzerland — 6
   Environment and Best Chance to Visit — 9
   Social Bits of knowledge — 11

Chapter 1: Planning Your Trip — 15
   Fundamental Travel Data — 15
   Visa Requirements and Entry — 19
   Cash and Cash Matters — 22
   Language and Communication — 25
   Making the Ideal Schedule — 29
   Length of Stay — 34
   Travel Budgeting — 38
   Going with Family — 42
   Getting to Switzerland — 47
   Entry Requirements and a Visa — 50

Chapter 2: Exploring Coastal Charms — 53
   Lake Geneva and Its Marvels — 55

Chapter 3: Uncovering Hidden Gems — 59
   Adventures in the Swiss Countryside — 61
   The Jura Mountains — 65
   Lavaux Grape plantations — 68
   Gruyères and Its Cheddar — 71
   Emmental Region — 74
   Noteworthy Towns and Social Fortunes — 77

Chapter 4: Family-Friendly Escapes	**81**
Kid well-being and Medical care	84
Educational Activities	88
Chapter 5: Embracing Adventure Activities	**93**
Chapter 6: Taking full advantage of Your Outing	**98**
Dining in Switzerland	101
Eating Decorum	105
Options for Accommodation	109
Chapter 7: Navigating Swiss Transportation	**113**
Tips for Safety and Well-Being	116
Emergency Contacts	121
Travel Protection	124
Chapter 8: Packing Tips and Travel Checklist	**129**
Valuable Expressions and Language Guide	133

Introduction

Welcome to the captivating universe of Switzerland, where snow-capped magnificence meets the quiet appeal of beachfront locales. This timeless land, located in the center of Europe, has landscapes that are both awe and tranquility. It's where flawless lakes sparkle underneath transcending tops, where memorable towns murmur stories of hundreds of years past, and where experiences proliferate for the courageous voyager.

The Switzerland Travel Guide 2023-2024 is your identification to investigating this enthralling country, an objective that consistently mixes waterfront attractions, unlikely treasures, and family-accommodating breaks. Switzerland beckons with its diverse offerings, whether you're an avid adventurer, a cultural connoisseur, or a family looking for memorable experiences.

You are invited on a journey through Switzerland's coastal towns in this meticulously crafted guide, where historic treasures can be found at every turn and the shores of Lake Geneva sparkle in the sunlight. Cross the beautiful scenes of the Swiss open country, finding stowed away fortunes and relishing valid encounters. For families, there's an organized determination of youngster-supported undertakings that will make enduring recollections. What's more, if you're an adrenaline searcher, the Swiss Alps stand prepared to challenge your cutoff points with plenty of exciting exercises.

However, this guide isn't just about the places to go; it's about the excursion. As you turn these pages, you'll track down important bits of knowledge, nearby tips, and suggestions to assist with arranging the Switzerland experience of your fantasies. From reasonable travel data and convenience choices to feasting joys and transportation bits of knowledge, this guide takes care of you.

Switzerland is more than just a place to go; it's an encounter ready to be embraced. It's the way Swiss chocolate melts in your mouth, the fresh mountain air invigorates you, and history whispers in every narrow alley. It's the excitement of a flawless slant under your skis, the chuckling of your kids as they find another world and the feeling of miracle as you look at stunning scenes.

In this way, whether you're a carefully prepared explorer or leaving on your absolute first experience, dig into the pages of the Switzerland Travel Guide 2023-2024 and set out on an excursion of disclosure and pleasure. Switzerland is holding on to greet you wholeheartedly, and this guide is your vital aspect for opening its vast miracles. Here's where your Swiss adventure begins.

1. Getting to Know Switzerland

Overview Switzerland's diverse landscapes, historic towns, and family-friendly charm captivate visitors to the continent's center. The nation flaunts superb Snow-capped tops and tranquil waterfront areas, ideal for unwinding or experiencing. Notable towns like Zurich and Lucerne mix with unexpected, yet invaluable treasures and family-accommodating exercises.

Switzerland's social extravagance, from language variety to culinary practices, adds profundity to its appeal. With adrenaline-siphoning undertakings and remarkable encounters, Switzerland welcomes voyagers, everything being equal, to investigate its fortunes. Switzerland's Geography and Regions The geography of Switzerland is a symphony of stunning contrasts. Arranged in the core of Europe, it's a landlocked country prestigious for its noteworthy variety. Four distinct geographical regions make up the nation:

1. Switzerland's Plateau: Otherwise called the Focal Level, this locale involves about 33% of Switzerland's property region. With its delicately moving slopes and fruitful fields, it's the most crowded region of the country. Significant urban areas like Zurich, Bern, and Basel call this locale home. Voyagers will track down a mix of metropolitan complexity and rustic appeal, making it a fantastic base for investigation.

2. The Alps of the Jura: The Jura Mountains are a region with lush forests, rolling hills, and picturesque valleys to the northwest. The Jura offers quietness, ideal for climbers and nature devotees. Additionally, it is well-known for its charming watchmaking towns.

3. The Swiss Alps: The southern region of the country is dominated by the iconic Swiss Alps. This grand mountain range is a jungle gym for outside devotees all year. The Swiss Alps are a haven for mountaineering, hiking, and skiing, with everything from the Matterhorn's jagged beauty to the towering peaks of the Bernese Oberland.

4. Switzerland's Plateau: Ticino, Switzerland's Italian-speaking canton, is located in the Southern Alps, the southernmost region. It's a Mediterranean heaven, with palm-bordered lakeshores, enchanting towns, and a rich Italian impact.

Past these four essential locales, Switzerland is prestigious for its unblemished lakes, the biggest being Lake Geneva, Lake Constance, and Lake Lucerne. Each adds to Switzerland's amazing regular magnificence.

Exploring this different scene is a basic piece of any Swiss experience. Whether you look for the clamoring urban areas, the peaceful open country, or the levels of the Alps, Switzerland's geology offers something for each explorer to find.

Environment and Best Chance to Visit

Switzerland encounters a changed environment because of its different geological districts. The country's environment can be comprehensively arranged into four seasons:

1. Spring (Walk to May): Spring in Switzerland brings a feeling of recharging. The landscapes come to life with vibrant flowers as the temperatures begin to rise. This is a magnificent time for nature strolls, investigating urban areas, and appreciating outside exercises without the late spring swarms.

2. From June to August, summer: Switzerland's mid-year is warm and bright, making it a superb traveling season. Particularly in metropolitan areas and lower-altitude regions, temperatures can range from pleasantly warm to scorching. Summer is ideal for climbing in the Alps, swimming in the unblemished lakes, and going to different comprehensive developments and celebrations.

3. Fall (September to November): As the leaves change, autumn paints Switzerland gold, red, and orange. The weather conditions stay charming in early pre-winter yet slowly become cooler. This is an extraordinary time for climbing, wine sampling in grape plantations, and partaking in the delightful scenes.

4. Winter: November through February During this time of year, Switzerland is a winter wonderland. Snow covers the Swiss Alps, attracting skiers and snowboarders from all over the world. Famous ski resorts like Zermatt, Verbier, and St. Moritz wake up. Christmas markets, comfortable chalets, and winter sports make it an otherworldly opportunity to visit. Depending on your interests, the best time to visit Switzerland is when:

- Ski Aficionados: From mid-December to late March, ski resorts and winter sports are at their best.
- Outside Experiences: The mild weather of spring and early autumn is ideal for hiking, biking, and exploring the countryside.
- Social and City Voyagers: Summer is great for city visits, as you can appreciate outside exercises and social celebrations.

Switzerland's different environment guarantees that there's something to appreciate all year. The seasons you choose should correspond to the things you want to do and experience.

Social Bits of knowledge

Switzerland, with its rich social embroidery, offers a dazzling mix of customs, dialects, and impacts. Here are a few vital social bits of knowledge to upgrade how you might interpret this multi-layered country:

1. Diversity in Languages: Switzerland flaunts four authority dialects: German, French, Italian, and Romansh. The language expressed changes by the district. For instance, the central and eastern regions are dominated by German, the west by French, the south by Italian, and some parts of the Engadin Valley by Romansh. Learning a couple of fundamental expressions in the neighborhood language can improve your movement experience.

2. Timekeeping Ability: Switzerland is famous for its dependability. Swiss trains, transports, and public administrations stick to exact timetables. It's standard to be on time for arrangements and gatherings, so embrace the Swiss devotion to practicality during your visit.

3. Food Delights: Swiss food is affected by its adjoining nations. Customary dishes like fondue, raclette, and rösti are culinary staples. Embrace the chance to relish Swiss chocolate and cheddar, famous overall for their quality and flavor.

4. Celebrations and Festivals: Switzerland has plenty of celebrations and occasions all year. The Basel Fair, Fête de l'Escalade in Geneva, and the Locarno Film Celebration are only a couple of models. Taking part in neighborhood festivities gives a brief look into Swiss culture.

5. Alpine Culture: There is a rich tapestry of Alpine customs in mountainous regions. Folk music, alphorn playing, and yodeling are among these. Going to a customary Swiss society celebration or hearing an Alphorn execution is a wonderful social encounter.

6. Diplomacy and neutrality: Switzerland has a long history of diplomacy and is known for its neutrality. Find out about its obligation to harmony by visiting organizations like the Unified Countries Office in Geneva and the Red Cross Exhibition Hall.

7. Swiss Accuracy and Craftsmanship: Switzerland is known for its accuracy and craftsmanship, most strikingly in watchmaking and banking. You might want to take a look at watch museums and boutiques to learn more about the craftsmanship that goes into Swiss timepieces.

8. Regard for Nature: Swiss culture puts major areas of strength regarding the climate. The Swiss have a profound association with nature, and you'll find very much kept up with climbing trails, preservation endeavors, and unblemished scenes all through the country.

Your journey through Switzerland will be enhanced by embracing these cultural insights, allowing you to connect with locals and appreciate the country's diverse heritage. Whether you're investigating urban communities or drenching yourself in snow-capped towns, Switzerland's social variety is a steady wellspring of interest and disclosure.

Chapter 1: Planning Your Trip

Arranging an excursion to Switzerland is an interesting undertaking, as this dazzling High country offers an abundance of normal excellence, social encounters, and open-air experiences. It is essential to plan carefully to guarantee a pleasant and memorable journey. Here is a thorough manual to assist you with beginning:

Fundamental Travel Data

Before you set out on your excursion to Switzerland, having a thorough comprehension of fundamental travel information is urgent. These particulars will assist in ensuring a pleasant journey:

1. Currency: Switzerland's true cash is the Swiss Franc (CHF). Although credit cards are widely accepted, carrying cash is a good idea for small purchases and places that do not accept cards.

2. Zone time: Central European Time (CET), also known as UTC+1, is the time zone in Switzerland.

During sunshine saving time (from the last Sunday in Spring to the last Sunday in October), it follows the Focal European Mid-year (CEST), UTC+2.

3. Plugs: Switzerland uses outlets of type J. The standard frequency is 50 Hz and the voltage is 230 V. Voltage converters and plug adapters may be required by international travelers.

4. Connectivity on the go: Switzerland has incredibly versatile organization inclusion. For cost-effective options, think about purchasing a local SIM card or contacting your provider to inquire about your international roaming plan.

5. Crisis Numbers: In the event of crises, dial 112 for general crises or 117 for police help.

6. Drinking Water: Regular water in Switzerland is protected from drinking and is of superior grade. You can fill your reusable water bottle from wellsprings tracked down in many urban areas and towns.

7. Language: Switzerland has four authority dialects: German, French, Italian, and Romansh. The language expressed fluctuates by district, so it's useful to gain proficiency with a couple of fundamental expressions in the nearby language of the area you're visiting.

8. Tipping: It is standard however not mandatory to Tip in Switzerland. If service is not included, it is common practice in restaurants to round the bill or leave a 5- to 10-percent tip. For different administrations, similar to taxi rides, it is valued to gather together the admission.

9. Travel Protection: Exceptionally fitting to have travel protection cover health-related crises, trip abrogations, and other unanticipated circumstances. Guarantee your protection is legitimate for Switzerland.

10. Wellbeing Insurances: Switzerland is by and large a protected objective wellbeing-wise. No particular vaccinations are required. Notwithstanding, having travel protection that covers health-related emergencies is fitting.

11. Shopping Hours: Most shops and stores are open from 9 AM to 6:30 PM, with a break for lunch from 12 PM to 1:30 PM. A few stores and corner shops might have expanded hours.

12. Regulations for Customs: Find out more about Switzerland's traditions and guidelines regarding what you can bring into the country. Certain things, like tobacco and liquor, may have limits.

13. Public Bathrooms: Switzerland has a lot of public restrooms. Access may require a small fee in some instances.

14. Transportation Tickets: The public transportation system in Switzerland is effective, but it can be costly. Consider buying a Swiss Travel Pass for limitless travel on open transportation and a limited section to attractions.

15. Safety: Switzerland is known for its security. While it's for the most part protected, it's wise to practice standard precautionary measures, for example, shielding your effects and monitoring your environmental factors, particularly in traveler regions.

Visa Requirements and Entry

Before planning your trip to Switzerland, it is essential to comprehend the entry requirements and visa requirements. Here is an itemized outline to assist you with exploring this part of your excursion:

1. Visa Exclusions: Switzerland is essential for the Schengen Region, a gathering of European nations with open lines and a typical visa strategy. For short visits of up to 90 days within 180 days, you typically do not require a visa if you are a citizen of a Schengen member state or a country that has a visa waiver agreement with Switzerland. These visa-absolved nations incorporate the US, Canada, Australia, and numerous others. In any case, if it's not too much trouble, check the most recent necessities before your outing.

2. Visa Types: On the off chance that you're arranging a long-term visit, for example, for work, study, or family get-together, you should apply for a particular visa, contingent upon your motivation. Tourist visas, student visas, work visas, and family reunion visas are all common types of visas.

3. Schengen Visa: On the off chance that you require a visa to enter Switzerland, you'll regularly apply for a Schengen Visa, which permits you to visit all Schengen Region nations. This visa must be applied for at the Swiss embassy or consulate in your home nation.

4. Application for Visa: To apply for a Swiss visa, you'll have to finish an application structure, give a substantial identification, identification measured photographs, travel schedule, verification of convenience, evidence of monetary means to cover your visit, travel protection, and different records relying upon your visa type.

5. Handling Time: Visa handling times can shift, so it's fitting to apply well ahead of your movement date, preferably no less than 90 days to come.

6. Section and Customs: You will have to go through customs and border control when you get to Switzerland. Guarantee you have all necessary reports prepared for assessment. Your identification ought to be legitimate for somewhere around 90 days past your planned flight date from Switzerland.

7. Section Stamps: Switzerland doesn't regularly stamp identifications of Schengen Region voyagers upon passage. Instead, you might be given a stamp on a separate sheet of paper, which you should keep with your passport during your stay.

8. Overstaying: Be aware of your allowed length of stay (normally 90 days inside a 180-day time frame). Exceeding can bring about fines, extradition, or future passage limitations.

9. Permits for Residence: If you intend to remain in Switzerland long haul, you'll have to apply for a home license once you show up. Whether you are applying for a residence permit for work, school, or family reunification, the requirements and procedures vary depending on your situation.

10. Renewals: On the off chance that you've conceded a home grant, know about its termination date and any restoration necessities. Without a valid permit, staying in Switzerland can result in legal problems.

Cash and Cash Matters

While going to Switzerland, it's fundamental to comprehend the nation's cash and cash-related perspectives to guarantee a smooth and effortless monetary experience during your outing. Here is an inside and out see money, banking, and spending contemplations:

1. Swiss Franc (CHF): The authority money of Switzerland is the Swiss Franc (CHF). The image for the Swiss Franc is "CHF," and it is frequently shortened to "Fr."

2. Coins and Banknotes: There are a variety of denominations for Swiss Franc banknotes, including 10,

20, 50, 100, 200, and 1,000 CHF. Coins are given in categories of 5, 10, and 20 centimes, as well as 1, 2, and 5 Francs.

3. Cash Trade: You can trade your home cash for Swiss Francs at banks, money trade workplaces, or ATMs (computerized teller machines) all through Switzerland. Cash trade workplaces are regularly found at air terminals, train stations, and significant traveler regions. Know that trade rates might shift marginally among various suppliers.

4. ATM Access: ATMs are well-established in Switzerland. You can pull out Swiss Francs from ATMs utilizing your charge or Visa. Check with your bank about global withdrawal charges to advance your utilization.

5. Charge cards: Credit and charge cards are broadly acknowledged in Switzerland, particularly in metropolitan regions and well-known vacationer locations. The most frequently accepted cards are American Express and Diners Club, followed by Visa and MasterCard. It's really smart to convey a little money for more modest organizations and provincial regions.

6. Apps for converting currencies: Consider introducing cash change applications on your cell phone to remain refreshed on trade rates and pursue informed monetary choices.

7. Shopping and Expenses: The majority of goods and services in Switzerland are subject to Value Added Tax (VAT), which is included in the prices that are displayed. Guests living external Switzerland can frequently guarantee a Tank discount on specific buys while withdrawing from the country. Make certain to ask about tax-exempt shopping choices at taking part stores and solicit the fundamental desk work for a discount.

8. Planned spending: Switzerland is known for its significant expense of living, so it's fundamental for financial planning in like manner. Make a budget for costs associated with activities, dining, lodging, and transportation. Research reasonable eating choices like neighborhood bistros and markets to oversee costs.

9. Unfamiliar Trade Administrations: If you have extra Swiss Francs toward the finish of your outing, you can trade them back into your home money at cash trade workplaces or banks.

By grasping the cash, installment strategies, and monetary contemplations in Switzerland, you can settle on informed choices to guarantee an agreeable and pleasant visit. Continuously advise your bank or Mastercard organization of your itinerary items to keep away from any unforeseen issues with your cards while abroad.

Language and Communication

Switzerland is a country with a lot of different languages and is multilingual. To get the most out of your trip, it's helpful to know the languages spoken, how to communicate, and how to have successful interactions:

1. Languages of Government: Switzerland's diverse culture and regions are reflected in its four official languages. These dialects are German, French, Italian, and Romansh. Every language prevails in unambiguous regions:

- The central and eastern regions, including Zurich, Bern, and Lucerne, are dominated by the spoken language of German, which is the most widely spoken.
- French is spoken in the western piece of Switzerland, especially in urban communities like Geneva and Lausanne.
- Italian is the authority language in the southern locale of Ticino and a few regions around Lake Geneva.

A lesser-known language in eastern Switzerland is Romansh, which is spoken in a few Alpine valleys.

2. English Capability: Even though most Swiss speak their native language well, English is widely spoken, especially in cities and tourist destinations. You'll track down that numerous Swiss individuals, especially those functioning in the travel industry, can convey serenely in English.

3. Greetings: While communicating with local people, a pleasant hello is valued. In German-talking regions, say "Guten Tag" (Great day), in French-talking regions, use "Bonjour," and in Italian-talking areas, say "Buongiorno." A basic "Hi" functions admirably in English.

4. Punctuality: Swiss culture puts areas of strength on dependability. On the off chance that you have an arrangement or reservation, show up on time. It is impolite to be late, even by a few minutes.

5. Language Software: Consider utilizing language applications or conveying a pocket phrasebook to assist you with fundamental expressions in the neighborhood dialects. Even though English is used a lot, it's appreciated to try to speak the language.

6. Multilingual Signage: Signage, particularly in transportation centers and traveler regions, is commonly in numerous dialects, including English, so you will not experience difficulty exploring.

7. Swiss German: In German-talking districts, the nearby vernacular can be trying to comprehend. Most Swiss Germans can change to standard High German or English for correspondence with non-German speakers.

8. Politeness: Swiss individuals esteem amenability and may utilize formal language (Sie in German, Vous in French) while meeting outsiders. It's an honorable gesture. Give back in kind, except if the other individual recommends utilizing casual language (Du in German, Tu in French).

9. Communication without speaking: In Swiss culture, nonverbal cues like maintaining eye contact, giving a firm handshake, and speaking with moderation are valued.

10. Tipping: Tipping customs vary, but they are typically less prevalent than in some other nations. Gathering together the bill or adding a little tip (around 5-10%) is standard in cafés and for administrations like taxi rides.

11. Services for Emergencies: The emergency services hotline in Switzerland is 117 (Swiss-specific) or 112 (available throughout Europe). Administrators commonly communicate in various dialects, including English.

Making the Ideal Schedule

Planning a very much organized schedule is vital to capitalizing on your Switzerland trip. Whether you're arranging seven days in a lengthy get-away or a long-term visit, here are the moves toward making an ideal schedule custom-fitted to your inclinations:

1. Characterize Your Objectives

Begin by setting clear goals for your excursion. What is it that you need to encounter in Switzerland? Is it climbing in the Swiss Alps, investigating memorable towns, or enjoying culinary joys? Your itinerary will be guided by your priorities.

2. Research Objections

Switzerland offers a large number of encounters, from cosmopolitan urban communities to quiet mountain towns. Research various locales and their attractions to match your inclinations. Take into account well-known destinations like Lucerne, Zurich, Interlaken, and the Jungfrau Region, as well as lesser-known gems.

3. Span of Stay

Decide how long you'll be in Switzerland. While it's enticing to cover the whole nation, center around unambiguous locales in light of your accessible time. The convenient transportation system in Switzerland makes exploring various regions simple.

4. Everyday Exercises

Separate your outing step by step. Settle on exercises, trips, and touring. Include activities in the great outdoors, cultural encounters, must-see landmarks, and time for relaxation. Avoid overscheduling; take into consideration adaptability.

5. Find a Balance in Your Trip

Make progress toward a fair blend of encounters. Combine sightseeing in the city with trips to the countryside, historic landmarks with modern attractions, and active adventures with leisurely breaks. Switzerland's variety takes care of different interests.

6. Travel Coordinated operations

Plan how you'll move between objections. Swiss public transportation is amazing, with trains, cable cars, transports, and boats covering the whole country. The Swiss Travel Pass can improve your movement game plans.

7. Accommodations

Pick facilities decisively. Remain in downtown areas for simple admittance to metropolitan attractions or in mountain chalets for a serene encounter. Think about inns, guesthouses, or Airbnb rentals, contingent upon your inclinations and spending plan.

8. Dining encounters:

Swiss cuisine is a delightful combination of flavors from neighboring nations. Try regional specialties like fondue, raclette, and rösti at meals at local establishments. Remember to appreciate Swiss chocolates and cheeses.

9. Climate Contemplations

Switzerland's weather conditions differ via season and district. Check weather conditions estimates for your movement dates and pack as needed. Plan open-air exercises during positive atmospheric conditions.

10. Reservations and Tickets

To guarantee your spot at popular excursions and attractions, book tickets and reservations in advance. This is especially crucial for activities like guided tours and mountain cable cars.

11. Far-reaching developments

Research widespread developments, celebrations, and displays occurring during your visit. You can learn more about Swiss customs and enhance your experience by attending local celebrations.

12. Budgeting

Foster a financial plan to monitor costs. Plan because Switzerland can be pricey. Consider buying city cards or passes for limits on attractions and transportation.

13. Remain Adaptable

While it's fundamental to have an organized schedule, take into consideration immediacy. Give yourself some time to unanticipatedly discover new things and unwind.

14. Crisis Contacts

Keep a rundown of fundamental contacts, remembering your nation's international haven or department for Switzerland, nearby crisis numbers, and your convenience subtleties.

Length of Stay

Settling on the span of your visit to Switzerland is a basic part of arranging your outing. The length that's right for you depends on your interests, where you want to go, and what you want to experience. Here is a top-to-bottom manual to assist you with deciding the proper length of stay for your Swiss experience:

1. The Seven to Ten-Day "Classic" Swiss Tour

On the off chance that you're a first-time guest or wish to cover the notorious Swiss objections, a 7-10 road trip is a phenomenal beginning stage. You will be able to experience the essentials during this time:

- **2-3 days in Zurich:** Take in the vibrant culture, museums, and shopping of the largest city in Switzerland.
- **2-3 days in Lucerne:** Find the beguiling city, visit Lake Lucerne, and access the close by Swiss Alps.
- **Two to three days in Interlaken:** Appreciate experience exercises in the Jungfrau Area, including climbing and mountain trips.
- **2-3 days in Zermatt:** Witness the lofty Matterhorn, investigate the hotel town, and participate in elevated experiences.
- **1-2 days in Geneva or Lausanne:** Experience the magnificence of Lake Geneva and its environmental factors.

2. Extensive exploration for at least 10 to 14 days

For a more top-to-bottom insight, consider an outing lasting 10-14 days or more. This permits you to dive further into every locale, take part in comfortable investigation, and consolidate extra objections:

- For a more leisurely pace, spend an additional day in Zermatt, Lucerne, Interlaken, or Zurich.
- Investigate Swiss wine areas like the Lavaux Grape plantations close to Lausanne.
- Devote time to less popular towns and districts like Basel, Bern, or the Valais canton.

3. Specialized Activities and Interests

On the off chance that you have explicit interests, like skiing, climbing, social drenching, or food and wine encounters, your length of stay might fluctuate. Ski fans could settle on seven days in a Swiss ski resort, while devoted climbers could design a lengthy visit to investigate grand paths.

4. Relaxed Immersion: Two to Four Weeks

Consider staying anywhere from two to four weeks for a truly immersive experience and the chance to learn about various aspects of Swiss life. This permits you to:

- Visit both notable and off in unexpected direction objections.

- Take part in neighborhood exercises, classes, or chipping in.
- Experience the change of seasons and different scenes.

5. Stays for longer than a few months:

Longer stays of 1-3 months or more are possible for expatriates, students, and remote workers who want to connect more deeply with Switzerland. You can:

Lay out a transitory home and investigate Switzerland as a nearby.

Immerse yourself in Swiss culture, pick up the language, and make connections that matter.

Eventually, the length of your visit to Switzerland ought to line up with your movement objectives, interests, and the encounters you want. From its stunning natural landscapes to its rich cultural heritage, Switzerland offers a wealth of opportunities to create lasting memories, regardless of duration.

Travel Budgeting

Because of its pristine landscapes and high standard of living, travelers may be concerned about the cost of visiting Switzerland. While it is the case that Switzerland can be costly, cautious preparation and planning can assist you with capitalizing on your excursion without burning through every last cent. A comprehensive budgeting guide for your trip to Switzerland is provided below:

1. Accommodation

The costs of lodging can vary greatly based on your choices. Switzerland provides a variety of choices, including budget hostels, vacation rentals, and luxury hotels.

- Low-cost lodging options like hotels and guesthouses: Prices range from about $40 to $80 per night.
- **Mid-Reach Lodgings:** Expect to spend between $120 and $300 per night.

- **Lavish Lodgings and Resorts:** Costs can surpass $400 each evening.
- Consider remaining in family-run hotels or guesthouses for a genuine involvement with a sensible expense.

2. Dining

- Eating out in Switzerland can be expensive, but there are ways to cut costs:
- **Eateries Nearby:** Choose nearby eateries, bistros, and road sellers to moderately test Swiss cooking.
- **Self-Catering and Supermarkets:** Enjoy picnics or cook your meals if your lodging permits. Shop for groceries at supermarkets.
- **Extraordinary Treats:** Aim for a few unique dining experiences and set aside money for them.

3. Transportation

Switzerland's extensive and effective public transportation system is a major draw. Consider these transportation costs:

- **Swiss Passport:** On the off chance that you intend to investigate numerous locales, a Swiss Travel Pass can be practical, covering trains, transports, cable cars, and even boats.
- **Tickets from Point to Point:** On the off chance that you have explicit objections as a main priority, buy individual tickets depending on the situation.
- **Car letting:** On the off chance that you favor adaptability and plan to visit distant regions, think about leasing a vehicle, however, consider fuel, costs, and leaving charges.

4. Touring and Exercises

Switzerland offers different exercises, from climbing and skiing to historical center visits and picturesque train rides. The spending plan for these encounters is given your inclinations.

Search for vacationer passes that proposition limits on attractions and exercises.

5. Incidental Costs

Remember to apportion assets for unexpected costs, trinkets, and travel protection.

6. Savings Tips

Exploit free exercises like climbing and investigating beguiling towns.

- Buy a Swiss Rail Half Toll Card for half limits on most trains, transports, cable cars, and mountain streetcars.
- For more information about the Swiss Travel System's tickets and pricing, visit their official website.
- Go on vacation during the shoulder seasons, which are spring and autumn, to get better prices.

7. Cash Trade:

Switzerland utilizes the Swiss Franc (CHF). For the best exchange rates, use an ATM or a bank.

Going with Family

Switzerland is an incredible objective for family travel, offering a wide exhibit of exercises and attractions reasonable for all ages. Here is an extensive aide on the most proficient method to design and partake in a critical vacation to Switzerland:

1. Picking Family-Accommodating Objections

Select destinations that cater to a variety of family interests as a starting point. The cities of Zurich, Lucerne, Interlaken, and Zermatt offer a variety of cultural and outdoor activities that are suitable for both adults and children.

2. Options for Accommodation

- You might want to think about staying in family-friendly places like serviced apartments, resorts with kid's clubs, or hotels with connecting rooms.
- Search for inns that give conveniences like play regions, dens, and keeping an eye on.

3. Attractions and Activities

Switzerland flaunts various family-accommodating exercises and attractions:

- **Mountain Undertakings:** Appreciate trolley rides to high-height regions, where you can investigate climbing trails, visit snow-capped jungle gyms, and take in stunning perspectives.
- **The Swiss Attractions:** Plan visits to carnivals like Swissminiatur, Jungfraupark, or Connyland.
- **Intelligent Galleries:** Investigate active exhibition halls like the Swiss Gallery of

Transport, the Swiss Public Gallery, and the Swiss Science Community Technorama.

- **Meeting Animals:** Visit untamed life parks and zoos like Zurich Zoo and Tierpark Goldau.
- **Boat Outings:** Take beautiful boat rides on Switzerland's flawless lakes.
- **Tours of Chocolate and Cheese:** Participate in tours with Swiss chocolate and cheese-making activities for children.

4. Dining That Is Safe for Kids

Swiss cafés are by and large inviting to families, however, pick kid well-disposed restaurants while eating out.

- Look for establishments that have a children's menu or smaller portions.
- Swiss cooking incorporates dishes like cheddar fondue, rosti, and raclette that kids might appreciate.

5. Wellbeing and Wellbeing

Switzerland is a protected objective for families, however, forever be aware of traffic while investigating urban communities.

Make certain that your family has travel insurance that will cover any unanticipated health problems.

6. Language and Correspondence

The majority of Swiss people speak more than one language, and English is widely spoken in tourist areas. In any case, learning fundamental Swiss German or French phrases can be useful.

Download interpretation applications for accommodation.

7. Packing Tips

Bring fundamental things for youngsters, including open-to apparel, layers for fluctuating weather patterns, sunscreen, and bug repellent.

Make certain that your children have appropriate footwear for exploring and hiking.

8. Keeping occupied while traveling

- Keep youngsters drawn in during ventures with books, games, and electronic gadgets.
- Swiss trains frequently have family compartments with play regions for youngsters.

9. Social Responsiveness:

Train your kids about Swiss traditions and manners to guarantee an aware way of behaving during your visit.

10. Taking in Local Festivals:

Check assuming that any nearby celebrations or occasions are occurring during your visit, as they can give interesting social encounters to the family.

From taking in the stunning landscapes of Switzerland to immersing oneself in the country's rich culture and traditions, the country has a plethora of family-friendly activities. By arranging great and taking into account your family's advantages and needs, you can make valued recollections together in this lovely high objective.

Getting to Switzerland

Switzerland is known for its shocking scenes, pleasant urban areas, and energetic culture. Arriving is a piece of the experience, and this is the way to make your excursion to Switzerland a consistent encounter:

By Air

1. Swiss Air terminals: Zurich Airport (ZRH), Geneva Airport (GVA), and EuroAirport Basel-Mulhouse-Freiburg (BSL/MLH/EAP) are among the numerous international airports in Switzerland. Zurich is the biggest and most active, offering broad flight associations.

2. Picking Your Air Terminal: Select an air terminal given your objective. The major gateways are the airports of Zurich and Geneva, which have excellent transportation links to various Swiss cities.

3. Non-stop Flights: Contingent upon your takeoff area, you might track down non-stop trips to Swiss urban communities. Significant carriers like Swiss Worldwide Aircrafts, Lufthansa, and English Aviation routes frequently work these courses.

4. Flights Connecting: Assuming no non-stop flights are accessible, consider associating through significant European centers like Frankfurt, Paris, or Amsterdam. Swiss urban communities are all around associated with these air terminals.

Via Train

1. European Rail Organization: Switzerland is prestigious for its effective and picturesque train framework. European urban communities like Paris, Milan, and Munich offer direct train associations with Swiss urban communities.

48

2. Rapid Trains: Board fast trains like the TGV Lyria or EuroCity for agreeable and quick excursions.

3. Swiss Passport: Consider the Swiss Travel Pass, which offers limitless travel on Switzerland's rail organization and public vehicles.

By Car

1. Driving Courses: On the off chance that you favor an excursion, you can head to Switzerland. The nation has kept up with thruways and line intersections from adjoining European nations.

2. Vignette: Buy a thruway vignette (cost sticker) at the boundary or service stations, permitting you to utilize Swiss interstates.

By Bus

1. Eurolines: Eurolines and other international bus companies offer routes to Swiss cities and frequently provide a low-cost means of transportation.

Entry Requirements and a Visa

1. Schengen Zone: Switzerland is important for the Schengen Zone. A Schengen visa may be required to enter the country, depending on your nationality. Take a look at the Swiss government office or department in your nation of origin for necessities.

2. Validity of a passport: Check to see that your passport still has validity for at least three months after the date you plan to leave.

Regulations and customs:

1. Currency: Swiss Franc (CHF) is the authority cash. Money trade administrations are promptly accessible at air terminals and banks.

2. Plugs: Type J outlets with a 50Hz frequency and a voltage of 230V are used in Switzerland. Bring appropriate connectors for your gadgets.

3. Zone time: Switzerland works on Focal European Time (CET), which is UTC+1, and Focal European Late spring (CEST) during sunshine saving, which is UTC+2.

Language: Swiss nationals communicate in four authority dialects: German, French, Italian, and Romansh. English is broadly figured out, particularly in vacationer regions.

Showing up in Switzerland: The airports in Switzerland provide excellent public transportation links to cities. You can utilize trains, cable cars, transports, and taxicabs to arrive at your last objective. Swiss effectiveness guarantees that your excursion to Switzerland will be all around as pleasant as the actual nation.

Travel Documentation: Make sure you have easy access to your passport, visa (if necessary), tickets for your flights, trains, and buses, and information about your lodging. Keep duplicates of these archives too.

Because of Switzerland's well-connected transportation infrastructure, you can choose the mode of transportation that best suits your needs and arrive in this Alpine paradise without any problems.

Chapter 2: Exploring Coastal Charms

Switzerland may be landlocked, however, it flaunts staggering lakes that rival any seaside objective. A preview of what to expect when visiting Switzerland's lake regions is as follows:

1. Lake Geneva (Lac Léman): Along the shores of Lake Geneva, take in the opulence of Geneva, the charm of Montreux, and the French flair of Evian-les-Bains. Investigate the shocking Chillon Palace, taste Swiss wine in Lavaux's grape plantations, and appreciate watersports on the perfect lake.

2. The Vierwaldstättersee in Lake Lucerne: Submerge yourself in history in Lucerne and set out on a grand boat stumble on Lake Lucerne. Visit the Swiss Gallery of Transport, investigate beautiful lakeside towns like Weggis, and climb the close by mountains.

3. Lake Zurich (Zürichsee): Zurich's energetic city life meets the serenity of Lake Zurich. Walk around the promenade, visit social diamonds like Kunsthaus Zurich, and take boat rides to lakeside towns like Rapperswil.

4. Lake Constance (Bodensee): Imparted to Germany and Austria, Lake Constance offers a blend of Swiss culture and shocking scenes. Visit the Zeppelin Museum in Friedrichshafen, the flower island of Mainau, and local restaurants that serve fresh fish.

5. Lake Thun (Thunersee) and Lake Brienz (Brienzersee): These two picturesque lakes can be found in the Bernese Oberland. Take boat cruises, visit Thun, a historic city, and the Lauterbrunnen Valley, which is nearby.

6. Lake Maggiore (Lago Maggiore): Cross into the Italian-talking part of Switzerland to encounter Lake Maggiore's appeal. Ascona, the charming town on the Brissago Islands, and the exquisite Mediterranean cuisine are all worth a visit.

7. Lake Neuchâtel (Lac de Neuchâtel): Explore Neuchâtel, a prestigious town renowned for its watchmaking heritage. The Laténium archaeological park is a must-see, as are the lakeside promenades and Swiss chocolate.

8. Lake Lugano (Lago di Lugano): Take boat rides on Lake Lugano and explore the Italianate city of Lugano. Appreciate Swiss-Italian cooking, visit the pleasant Morcote town, and investigate the lovely close by mountains.

These Swiss lakes offer dazzling regular magnificence as well as social extravagance, watersports, and a large number of exercises. Whether you look for unwinding, experience, or social encounters, Switzerland's lakes bring something to the table for each explorer.

Lake Geneva and Its Marvels

Lake Geneva, known as Lac Léman in French, is Switzerland's biggest lake and one of the most dazzling waterways in Europe. Surrounded by pleasant towns and upheld by the staggering Alps, this lake offers an abundance of marvels ready to be investigated:

1. Geneva: The city of Geneva, situated at the western tip of the lake, is a worldwide strategic center, lodging various global associations, including the Unified Countries and the Red Cross. Visit the renowned Jet d'Eau fountain, which rises 140 meters into the air, and the Old Town for a taste of humanitarian history. Also, explore the Red Cross Museum.

2. Montreux: The Montreux Jazz Festival, which takes place every year, has made this charming lakeside town famous. Walk around the bloom-lined promenade and visit Chillon Palace, a middle-aged stronghold set on a little island in the lake. It's where history and regular magnificence merge.

3. Lausanne: Lausanne, Switzerland's fourth-largest city, is elegantly perched on Lake Geneva's northern shore. Visit the Olympic Museum, the well-preserved Old Town, and the Gothic masterpiece that is the Cathedral of Notre Dame.

4. Vevey: Known as the "Nestlé Town" because of its relationship with the food goliath, Vevey is a great town to investigate. Respect the Goliath fork form implanted in the lake, honor the sculpture of Charlie Chaplin, and visit the Alimentarium, a food and nourishment gallery.

5. The Vineyards of Lavaux: The terraced grape plantations of Lavaux on the northern shores of Lake Geneva are a UNESCO World Legacy site. Take a comfortable climb or bicycle ride through these beautiful grape plantations, testing nearby wines en route.

6. Yvoire: While situated in France, the middle age town of Yvoire is in many cases remembered for Lake Geneva schedules. Its cobblestone roads, beguiling nurseries, and very much protected palace make a captivating air.

7. Water Sports and Travels: Lake Geneva offers sufficient chances for water sports like cruising, paddleboarding, and swimming. Take a journey to partake in the peaceful excellence of the lake and its environmental elements.

8. Lakeside Eating: Relish flavorful Swiss and French food in lakeside eateries. New fish, nearby wines, and stunning perspectives are on the menu.

9. Events and Festivals: Over time, Lake Geneva has different comprehensive developments, from live events to wine samplings, adding energetic varieties to your visit.

Lake Geneva is something other than a lake; it's a social and normal gold mine, offering a different scope of encounters that mix history, workmanship, and stunning views. Whether you're investigating the urban communities or climbing through grape plantations, this district has something to captivate each explorer.

Chapter 3: Uncovering Hidden Gems

Switzerland is brimming with hidden gems waiting to be discovered by daring travelers, even though Lake Geneva and the surrounding cities frequently steal the spotlight.

1. The Aletsch Icy mass: As the biggest ice sheet in the Alps, the Aletsch Glacial mass is a UNESCO World Legacy site offering unmatched normal magnificence. Climb or take a trolley to observe this cold miracle very closely.

2. Valley of Engadin: Settled in the eastern Swiss Alps, Engadin flaunts unblemished scenes, beguiling towns, and completely clear lakes. Try not to miss the dazzling Lake Sils and the dynamic town of St. Moritz.

3. Appenzell: a picturesque Swiss village that is well-known for its vibrant traditions, distinctive cheese culture, and vibrant houses. Investigate the enrapturing Appenzell locale and drench yourself in Swiss legends.

4. Valley of Lauterbrunnen: Lauterbrunnen Valley is a lush, green oasis surrounded by towering cliffs in the Bernese Oberland. Witness shocking cascades, including the renowned Staubbach Falls, and set out on beautiful climbs.

5. Gimmelwald: a tiny, car-free village in the Jungfrau region perched on a cliff's edge. It's an optimal base for climbing and offers amazing perspectives on the Eiger, Mönch, and Jungfrau mountains.

6. Van Creux: Frequently alluded to as Switzerland's Fabulous Gulch, this regular amphitheater cut by ice sheets is a geographical marvel. Take a hike to the edge for breathtaking views.

7. The Emmental, or Emmental cheese, rolling hills, and traditional farms are just a few things that make this idyllic area famous. Investigate the open country, visit a cheddar dairy, and enjoy true Swiss flavors.

8. Schwarzsee: This small mountain lake, which is close to Fribourg, is a peaceful haven with serene surroundings and is a great place to start hiking adventures.

9. The Swiss Public Park: Switzerland's just public park, arranged in the Engadin Valley, is a safe house for nature devotees. It has pristine landscapes and a wide range of wildlife.

10. Gruyères: The medieval town of Gruyères, which is famous for its cheese, is a charming place with cobblestone streets, a stunning castle, and the HR Giger Museum, which displays the works of famous artists.

Switzerland's lesser-known landscapes, customs, and culture can be glimpsed through these enigmatic gems. These off-the-beaten-path locations promise unforgettable experiences whether you're looking for scenic beauty, cultural encounters, or tranquil retreats.

Adventures in the Swiss Countryside

Switzerland's countryside is a playground for nature and outdoor enthusiasts, despite its bustling cities and tranquil lakeshores. Consider these delightful outings in the countryside:

1. Climbing and Journeying: Switzerland is an explorer's heaven, with a broad organization of trails taking care of all levels. Hike through alpine meadows in the Bernese Oberland, the Swiss National Park, or challenging routes in the Valais region.

2. Mountain bike riding and cycling: There are scenic cycling routes in the Swiss countryside for cyclists of all abilities. Lease a bicycle and investigate the Lavaux Grape plantation Porches, ride along the shores of Lake Geneva, or assume the difficult mountain trails of Graubünden.

3. Hot Air Swelling: Take off over the Swiss scene in a tourist balloon for an extraordinary viewpoint. Appreciate stunning perspectives on the Swiss Alps, beautiful towns, and immaculate lakes.

4. Horseback Riding: Find Switzerland's wide-open riding horse. The stunning Engadin Valley and the

Emmental's rolling hills are just two of the many regions where guided horseback riding tours are available.

5. Hang gliders and paragliding: Take to the skies for an adrenaline rush. The Jungfrau Region, Interlaken, and Lauterbrunnen are all popular destinations for paragliding.

6. Fishing: Project your line in one of Switzerland's unmistakable mountain lakes or waterways. Get a fishing license and take a shot at getting trout, roost, or scorch.

7. Swiss traditional farms: To get a sense of Swiss rural life, visit farms in operation. Partake in cheddar making in the Appenzell district or find out about economical agribusiness in the Emmental.

8. Nearby Celebrations: Embrace Swiss culture by going to conventional celebrations in the open country. There is always a celebration to attend, whether it be wine festivals in the Valais or alpine cattle descents in the Grisons.

9. Natural life Watching: Wildlife abounds in Switzerland's countryside. You can see ibex, chamois, marmots, and a variety of bird species by participating in guided wildlife tours.

10. Safaris for photography: Catch the magnificence of the Swiss wide open with a photography visit. You'll learn how to get the best shots and be guided to the best vantage points by knowledgeable guides.

11. Health Retreats: Numerous wide-open areas offer health withdraws, including yoga and reflection. Loosen up in peaceful environmental factors while restoring your body and brain.

Whether you're looking for action in the great outdoors, cultural immersion, or just a peaceful getaway into the great outdoors, Switzerland's countryside adventures promise unforgettable experiences. With its immaculate scenes, beguiling towns, and a feeling of quietness, the Swiss Wide Open welcomes voyagers to investigate and interface with the regular world.

The Jura Mountains

The Jura Mountains, which are in the western part of Switzerland, are a one-of-a-kind haven away from the bustling cities and popular tourist destinations. This is the very thing you want to be aware of when investigating this delightful area:

1. Overview: The Jura Mountains structure a characteristic line between Switzerland and France. This region is known for its delicate moving slopes, thick woods, and pleasant valleys. The Jura Mountains are a great place for a quiet getaway because they are less crowded than the Swiss Alps.

2. Climbing and Journeying: The Jura locale brings a broad organization of climbing trails reasonable for all levels. Whether you're a seasoned hiker or just a casual walker, some trails will take you through picturesque villages, pastures, and pristine forests. The Jura Peak Trail is a well-known significant distance course offering all-encompassing perspectives.

3. Skiing in the Cross-Country: In the colder time of year, the Jura Mountains become a cross-country skiing heaven. All around kept up with trails wind through snow-shrouded scenes, giving an amazing an open door to winter sports lovers.

4. Jurassic Park: Find the land miracles of the Jura Mountains, which date back a large number of years. Investigate limestone caves, like the Grottes de Vallorbe, and find out about the district's old history.

5. Neighborhood Cooking: Enjoy the distinct flavors of the Jura region's cuisine. Try smoked sausages, fondue, and "Tête de Moine" cheese. Vin Jaune, one of the distinctive wines produced by local wineries, is renowned for its complex and nutty flavor.

6. Lively Natural life: The Jura Mountains are home to an assortment of natural life, including deer, wild pigs, and various bird species. Birdwatchers will especially partake in the assorted avian populace tracked down in the locale.

7. Traditional communities: Investigate beguiling towns like St-Ursanne and Porrentruy, where middle-age design and a feeling of history transport you back in time. Visit historic churches, wander cobblestoned streets, and take in the culture of the area.

8. Jurapark Aargau: This nature park is devoted to saving the Jura's extraordinary scene and social legacy. It offers instructive projects and directed visits for guests keen on the area's regular and social history.

9. Outdoor Activities: As well as climbing and skiing, the Jura Mountains offer open doors for mountain trekking, horseback riding, and rock climbing. Outdoor enthusiasts will enjoy the diverse landscapes in the region, which makes it a great playground.

10. Star gazing: The Jura Mountains' lower light contamination levels make them an optimal area for stargazing. Appreciate crisp evenings and divine miracles in this serene setting.

The Jura Mountains give a quiet retreat to those looking for a more slow speed and a more profound association with nature and culture. The Jura Mountains in the center of Switzerland provide an experience that is truly enriching, whether you choose to hike scenic trails, savor the cuisine of the area, or explore historical villages.

Lavaux Grape plantations

Lavaux Grape plantations, settled along the northern shores of Lake Geneva in Switzerland, is a UNESCO World Legacy site known for its stunning terraced grape plantations and excellent wines. Investigate this beautiful wine locale, where hundreds of years of viticultural custom have made a scene of unmatched magnificence.

1. Stunning Terraces: The intricate network of stone-walled terraces that cascade down the Swiss Riviera's steep slopes is Lavaux's most distinctive feature. These porches are a design wonder, worked over hundreds of years to boost daylight openness for grape development.

2. Picturesque Magnificence: As you meander through the terraced grape plantations, you'll be blessed to receive clearing perspectives on Lake Geneva, the Alps, and enchanting towns. The terraces create a one-of-a-kind microclimate that is great for growing grapes and makes for a beautiful backdrop for leisurely walks.

Wine History

3. Traditions in Viticulture: Lavaux's grape plantations have been developed since Roman times, and the district's winemaking legacy is profoundly imbued in its way of life. Nearby winemakers invest heavily in delivering a portion of Switzerland's best wines.

4. Wine sampling: Various wineries and basements are dissipated all through Lavaux, inviting guests to test different wines, including Chasselas, the district's unique grape assortment. Schedule a wine tasting to learn about the winemaking process and enjoy the flavors of Lavaux.

Investigation and Exercises

5. Walking Routes: Lavaux offers an organization of very much-stamped climbing trails that breeze through the grape plantations. These trails are a great way to see the natural beauty of the area and find hidden treasures.

6. Wine Visits: If you want to learn more about Lavaux's terroir, winemaking methods, and the history of its vineyards, take a guided wine tour. Wine tastings are also a part of many tours.

Enchanting Towns

7. St-Saphorin: Investigate the beautiful town of St-Saphorin, with its archaic engineering, limited roads, and beguiling wine basements. The town gives a brief look into the district's rich history.

8. Rivaz: Visit Rivaz, another interesting town prestigious for its wine creation. You'll track down superb terraced gardens, old sanctuaries, and amicable local people anxious to share their adoration for winemaking.

Occasions and Celebrations

9. **Fête de l'Escalade:** Lavaux commends its wine culture with different occasions consistently. Wine tastings, music, and culinary delights are all part of the lively Fête de l'Escalade festival, which takes place in December.

Gruyères and Its Cheddar

Gruyères, a pleasant Swiss town settled in the Fribourg Alps, is famous overall for its eponymous cheddar, Gruyère. This enchanting objective offers a brilliant excursion into Swiss culinary practices and a rich social legacy.

The Cheese Gris

1. **Heritage of Cheese:** This region has been producing gruyère cheese for centuries. It is a cheese with a coveted protected designation of origin (AOP) that is firm, creamy, and slightly nutty.

2. Cheddar Dairies: Guests can investigate conventional cheddar dairies in Gruyères, where gifted craftsmen carefully follow age-old recipes to make this notable cheddar. Witness the cheddar-making process and find out about the thorough norms that guarantee the cheddar's quality.

Gruyères, France

3. Middle-age Appeal: The town of Gruyères is a residing postcard, with its middle-age engineering, cobblestone roads, and interesting houses. Take in the atmosphere of a bygone era as you stroll through its well-preserved historic center.

4. Château de Gruyères: Overwhelming the town's horizon is the Château de Gruyères, a radiant middle age palace. Investigate its exquisite lobbies, workmanship assortments, and manicured gardens, acquiring knowledge of the town's respectable history.

Gastronomic Joys

5. Cheddar Fondue: At one of the cozy restaurants in Gruyères, indulge in cheese fondue, the ultimate Swiss comfort food. Plunge pieces of newly prepared bread into a percolating pot of Gruyère and Emmental cheeses, joined by a glass of neighborhood white wine.

6. Raclette: Enjoy a quintessential Swiss dish, raclette, where a wheel of Gruyère cheddar is warmed, and its softened layer is scratched onto coffee shops' plates. It's a delightfully intuitive culinary experience.

Maison du Gruyère

7. Cheddar Experience: Through multimedia exhibits, learn about the cheese-making process at the interactive Maison du Gruyère dairy. Your tour will come to an end with cheese tastings, where you can try Gruyère at various stages of maturation.

Yearly Occasions

8. The Great Gourmet Rando: Participate in La Grande Rando Gourmande, a gourmet hike through the idyllic Fribourg countryside that features local products like Gruyère cheese, if you visit in September.

Gruyères is a dazzling objective where cheddar devotees and history buffs the same can delight in the craft of cheddar making, investigate a middle-aged town, and relish delicious Swiss dishes. If you spend some time learning about Gruyère cheese, you'll come away with a better understanding of Swiss cuisine.

Emmental Region

The Emmental region, which is located in the center of Switzerland, is a picturesque landscape that is well-known for its rolling hills, charming villages, and, most importantly, the Emmental cheese, which is well-known for its distinctive holes and is found all over the world. This locale offers a superb mix of regular excellence, culinary customs, and a beguiling legacy.

Emmental Cheddar

1. Heritage Emmental Cheese: Emmental cheddar, frequently perceived as "Swiss cheddar," has a set of experiences profoundly entwined with this district. Its unmistakable openings, or "eyes," are the sign of this eminent cheddar.

2. Making cheese: Guests can investigate nearby cheddar dairies where gifted cheesemakers create Emmental cheddar utilizing conventional strategies. Witness the cheddar-making process, from coagulating to maturing, and gain experience in the craft of cheddar creation.

The Emmental Region

3. Moving Slopes: The Emmental area is distinguished by its lush green hills, which are punctuated by charming farms and cows grazing. The scene is ideal for relaxed strolls or bicycle rides, offering stunning vistas every step of the way.

4. Emme Stream: The region's idyllic beauty is further enhanced by the Emme River's slithering course. Beautiful scaffolds and strolling ways give amazing chances to see the value in the peaceful waters and encompassing open country.

Legacy and Culture

5. Thun: It is worthwhile to pay a visit to the Emmental-border town of Thun. Take a stroll along the lakeside promenade, check out the medieval old town of Thun, and go to Thun Castle for stunning views of the surrounding area.

Culinary Enjoyments

6. Emmental Cooking: Emmental cheddar is at the core of the district's food. Enjoy Emmental cheese at its best in traditional Swiss dishes like raclette and cheese fondue.

7. Neighborhood Markets: To sample and purchase freshly made Emmental cheese and other regional products, visit dairy shops and local markets.

Emmental Nature Park

8. Nature Investigation: The Emmental Nature Park offers an opportunity to investigate the district's regular magnificence. Enjoy the region's biodiversity as you hike through pristine landscapes, meet native wildlife, and learn about it.

The Emmental district offers a dazzling mix of normal excellence, cheddar-making legacy, and Swiss practices. The Emmental region welcomes you to immerse yourself in its charm and flavors, whether you're a cheese lover, a nature lover, or just looking for a peaceful escape.

Noteworthy Towns and Social Fortunes

Switzerland isn't just honored with stunning scenes but also flaunts a rich history and energetic culture. In this part, we dive into a portion of the country's notable towns and social diamonds that offer explorers a brief look into its entrancing at various times.

Lucerne

1. Enchanting Old Town: Lucerne's very much protected old town is a storybook setting with cobblestone roads, middle-age design, and vivid frescoed structures. Investigate the famous Kapellbrücke (Sanctuary Scaffold) and walk around the Reuss Stream.

2. Social Features: Lucerne is home to list social scenes like the KKL Luzern (Culture and Conference Hall) and the Richard Wagner Historical Center. To get a taste of the local arts scene, go to an opera or classical music concert.

Bern

3. Middle age Excellence: Bern, the capital of Switzerland, is a city on the UNESCO World Heritage List with a stunningly preserved medieval old town. Explore the arcade-lined cobblestone streets beneath the recognizable Zytglogge clock tower.

4. Einstein's Heritage: The Einstein House is where Albert Einstein lived for a significant amount of time. In this historic setting, learn about the physicist's life and work.

Zurich

5. Craftsmanship and Exhibition halls: Zurich flaunts a flourishing expression scene with various historical centers and exhibitions. The Swiss National Museum provides insights into Switzerland's history, while the Kunsthaus Zurich houses an impressive collection of European art.

Geneva

6. Center for the World: Geneva is well-known for its international organizations, such as the Red Cross and the United Nations. Investigate the Worldwide Red Cross and Red Sickle Gallery and gain a more profound comprehension of philanthropic endeavors.

Lausanne

7. Olympic Legacy: The Olympic Museum is located in Lausanne, the Olympic capital. Find the historical backdrop of the Olympic Games and investigate intuitive shows committed to sports and competitors.

Park National de Suisse

8. Heritage of Nature: The Swiss National Park is important for its ecological and cultural significance, even though it is not a historic town. It is the only national park in Switzerland, where Alpine wildlife and pristine landscapes are protected. Explore the outdoors by hiking the marked trails.

Chapter 4: Family-Friendly Escapes

Switzerland is an incredible objective for families, offering a mix of outside undertakings, instructive encounters, and vital minutes. A brief overview of some family-friendly getaways is as follows:

1. Swiss Attractions: Switzerland has a few amusement stops that take special care of families. From the Swiss Vapeur Parc with its scaled-down steam trains to Jungfrau Park's dinosaur shows children, everything being equal, will find these parks enthralling.

2. Amusement Parks: Take part in exciting exercises at experience parks like Seilpark Interlaken or Rope Park Gantrisch. Challenge yourselves with treetop impediment courses, and ziplines, and that's just the beginning.

3. Animal Interactions: Zoos and natural life parks have large amounts in Switzerland. For a more in-depth look at native Swiss species, head to the Tierpark Goldau or the Zurich Zoo, both of which house animals from all over the world.

4. Swiss Chocolate Experiences: Swiss chocolate is amazingly popular, and kids (and grown-ups) will thoroughly enjoy chocolate-themed attractions like Maison Cailler close to Gruyères or the Chocolate Frey Guest Center.

5. Intuitive Historical centers: Family-friendly interactive exhibits can be found in Swiss museums. Kids can climb aboard vintage trains and vehicles at the Swiss Museum of Transport in Lucerne or the Technorama Science Center in Winterthur.

6. Alpine Excursions: Take your family to the Swiss Alps for climbing, skiing, or just partaking in the perfect mountain scenes. There are numerous family-friendly activities available throughout the year in places like Zermatt, Jungfrau, and the Engadin Valley.

7. Swiss Family Card: Families going with youngsters under 16 can profit from the Swiss Family Card, which gives free open transportation to kids when joined by no less than one parent with a Swiss Travel Pass.

8. Instructive Encounters: Switzerland's social and verifiable destinations frequently offer directed visits and studios custom-fitted to kids. It's a pleasant way for youngsters to find out about Swiss history and customs.

9. Lake Activities: Boat rides, swimming, and picnicking along the shores of Swiss lakes like Lakes Geneva, Lucerne, and Constance are all options.

10. Fun at Fondue: Try not to botch the opportunity to acquaint your children with Swiss fondue. Numerous cafés offer family-accommodating renditions of this messy joy.

Switzerland is a great place to spend time with loved ones and make lasting memories due to its natural beauty and family-friendly attractions. There is something for everyone in the family to enjoy, whether it's experiencing cultural events or the great outdoors.

Kid well-being and Medical care

Going with kids requires unique regard for their security and prosperity. Switzerland, known for its brilliant medical services framework and by and large wellbeing, is an ideal location for family excursions. Here is an aide on youngster security and medical care during your excursion:

1. Healthcare in the Swiss Alps

Switzerland flaunts a top-notch medical services framework. Clinics and centers are outfitted with present-day offices and staffed by profoundly prepared clinical experts. As a vacationer, you can get to medical care administrations if necessary. Having travel protection that covers health-related crises and repatriation is prudent. The crisis number in Switzerland is 112 for any earnest clinical help or crises.

2. Vaccinations

Travelers to Switzerland are generally exempt from specific vaccination requirements. Make certain that all of your children have received their routine vaccinations.

3. Safe Water

Switzerland's tap water is safe to drink. Convey reusable water bottles for your family to remain hydrated, particularly during open-air exercises.

4. Childproofing Facilities

While booking facilities, ask about childproofing choices. A few inns and lofts offer childproof rooms, including attachment covers and step entryways.

5. Vehicle Security

Switzerland has strict laws regarding car seats, so you should plan to rent one. Kids under 12 years of age or more limited than 150 cm (4'11") should utilize fitting kid seats. When booking your rental car, bring your child's car seat with you or inquire about renting one.

6. Traffic Wellbeing

Swiss streets are by and large protected, however consistently focus on traffic security. Be sure to teach your children to look both ways before crossing streets and to use designated pedestrian crossings. When cycling, a popular family activity in Switzerland, encourage helmet use.

7. Security in the outdoors

Switzerland offers innumerable outside exercises, including climbing and skiing. Make sure everyone in your family is wearing the right safety gear, especially if they are doing winter sports. Dress kids energetically in chilly climates and apply sunscreen during bright days, as the mountain sun can be extreme.

8. Services for Emergencies

The emergency services in Switzerland are prompt and effective. If your children get lost, teach them to call 112 or the authorities.

9. Neighborhood Decorum

Switzerland is a safe and polite country; however, it is essential to instruct your children in local protocol. Urge them to be aware of Swiss traditions and culture.

10. Restrictions on Diet and Allergies

Inform restaurants and other establishments in advance if your child has any allergies or dietary restrictions. Most Swiss establishments are hospitable.

11. Pharmacies

Drug stores (Apotheke) are generally accessible and very much supplied. They can give non-prescription meds and medical aid supplies.

12. Language Obstructions

Switzerland has numerous authority dialects. While most Swiss individuals communicate in English, it's useful to learn fundamental expressions in the nearby language of the area you're visiting.

Switzerland's obligation to somewhere safe and medical care guarantees that your family's prosperity is a main concern during your visit. By playing it safe and remaining informed, you can partake in a straightforward and critical excursion with your kids in this lovely country.

Educational Activities

Switzerland has a plethora of family-friendly educational activities that combine fun and education. Here are some improving exercises to connect with your youngsters while investigating this dazzling country:

1. Tours of the Swiss Chocolate Factory

Switzerland is prestigious for its heavenly chocolate. Take your family on a chocolate manufacturing plant visit like Nestle's Cailler factory in Broc or Toblerone's Bernese factory. Witness the chocolate-production process and taste some Swiss chocolate.

2. Swiss Workshops for Watchmaking

Switzerland is popular for its accurate watchmaking. Visit watch exhibition halls and studios, where children can find the multifaceted specialty of creating Swiss watches. A few significant offers involved watchmaking encounters.

3. Swiss Science Historical Centers

Swiss science galleries like the Swiss Vehicle Gallery in Lucerne or the Swiss Science Community Technorama in Winterthur give intuitive shows to youngsters to investigate different logical peculiarities and standards.

4. Snow-capped Untamed life Parks

Switzerland's High districts are home to assorted untamed life. Take your family to natural life parks like the Juraparc in Mont-d'Orzeires or the Wildpark Peter and Paul in St. Gallen to notice local creatures very close.

5. Visit Swiss Homesteads

Swiss homesteads offer an opportunity for youngsters to encounter country life. They can drain cows, feed animals, and find out about maintainable cultivating rehearses. Ranches like the Zugerberg in Zug or Tropenhaus Frutigen offer instructive visits.

6. Swiss Cheddar Dairies

Swiss cheddar is a culinary enjoyment. Visit cheddar dairies like Emmental Show Dairy in Affoltern or Appenzeller Cheddar Dairy to observe the cheddar-making cycle and relish newly made cheddar.

7. Nature Trails in the Alps

Switzerland's amazing scenes are ideal for instructive climbs. Elevated nature trails like the Blumenweg in Mürren or the Planets Trail in Engelberg offer enlightening billboards about greenery, fauna, and the planetary group.

8. Swiss Cultural Attractions

Investigate authentic locales like the Château de Chillon in Montreux or the Roman Historical Center in Augusta Raurica close to Basel. These locales give an understanding of Switzerland's rich history.

9. Tour Swiss Art Galleries

Swiss workmanship exhibition halls like the Fondation Beyeler in Basel or the Kunstmuseum in Zurich feature a different scope of fine arts. Encourage children's creativity and appreciation of art.

10. Snow-capped Greenhouses

Alpine plants and ecosystems are featured in botanical gardens like the University of Fribourg's Botanical Garden and the Botanischer Garten in Zurich. Kids can learn about Switzerland's unique flora.

11. Galactic Observatories

The Observatoire Astronomique de l'Université de Genève is one of several astronomical observatories in

Switzerland. Events for stargazing and education are frequently planned.

12. Learn Swiss Dialects

Switzerland has four authority dialects. Encourage your children to acquire fundamental phrases in the region's native language. Language submersion can be an instructive experience.

These instructive encounters in Switzerland animate interest as well as cultivate a more profound comprehension of Swiss culture, science, and nature. They join flawlessly with the nation's dazzling normal excellence, making learning an astonishing piece of your family's Swiss experience.

Chapter 5: Embracing Adventure Activities

Switzerland's dazzling scenes and outside potential open doors make it an undertaking darling's heaven. Here is a short outline of the outright exhilarating experience exercises you can appreciate in this Snow capped wonderland:

1. Climbing and Journeying

There are a lot of hiking trails in Switzerland. There is a trail for every level of hiker in the high Alps, from easy strolls to strenuous treks.

2. Snowboarding and skiing

Switzerland is an incredibly popular objective for winter sports. Whether you're a beginner or a specialist, the Swiss Alps offer perfect inclines and ski resorts.

3. Hang gliders and paragliding

Take off high over the Swiss scenes and appreciate amazing perspectives while paragliding or hang skimming.

4. Wilderness Boating

Assume the exhilarating rapids of Swiss streams like the Rhine and the Lütschine for an adrenaline-siphoning experience.

5. Biking the mountains

Investigate the Swiss wide open on very much checked mountain trekking trails. It's a great way to see the scenery, from easy rides to difficult descents.

6. Climbing Rocks

From challenging alpine routes to climbing gyms, Switzerland offers rock climbing opportunities for all levels.

7. Canyoning

Canyoning is a unique adventure sport that is popular in Switzerland. It allows you to descend through narrow gorges and waterfalls.

8. Climbing Ice

At the point when winter shows up, ice climbing lovers can handle frozen cascades and ice developments in the Swiss Alps.

9. Sledding and tobogganing

Experience the excitement of sledding down mountain inclines or partake in a relaxed sled ride with the family.

10. via a ladder

Test your climbing abilities on Swiss through Ferrata courses, which consolidate climbing and moving with got ways and iron rungs.

11. Amusement Parks

Experience parks like the Seilpark in Interlaken offers exciting rope courses and zip lines amid lovely normal settings.

12. Skydiving

Venture out with a skydiving experience, quickly dropping over Switzerland's stunning scenes.

13. Paddling and Kayaking

Paddle on immaculate Swiss lakes and streams, encompassed by staggering mountain landscapes.

14. Hot Air Swelling

Take off quietly over the Swiss field in a tourist balloon for a tranquil experience.

15. Caving

Wander through Switzerland's caverns and caves to discover the underground world's striking geological formations.

16. E-Biking

For an all the more comfortable trekking experience, attempt e-trekking to investigate panoramic detours easily.

Chapter 6: Taking full advantage of Your Outing

To guarantee your Switzerland experience is remarkable, here are a few critical ways to capitalize on your excursion:

1. Prepare Research: make an agenda that suits your inclinations and financial plan. Set a high priority on experiences and places to see.

2. Travel Protection: Secure complete travel protection to cover unforeseen occasions, including health-related crises and excursion scratch-offs.

3. Neighborhood Cooking: Test Swiss indulgences like fondue, raclette, and Swiss chocolate. Investigate nearby business sectors and eat at conventional Swiss cafés.

4. Learn the Basic Words: While numerous Swiss communicate in English, learning a couple of fundamental Swiss German or French expressions can upgrade your experience and recognize the neighborhood culture.

5. Public Transportation: Use Switzerland's proficient public transportation framework, including trains, cable cars, and transports. Consider a Swiss Travel Pass for limitless travel.

6. Preserve the Natural World: Switzerland is known for its immaculate scenes. Responsible tourism, including proper waste disposal and respect for wildlife, can aid in their preservation.

7. Follow the Rules: Follow neighborhood customs and guidelines, like calm hours and smoking limitations. Switzerland is known for its reliability, so be on time for visits and arrangements.

8. Cash The board: To avoid card issues, inform your bank of your travel plans and bring some Swiss Francs in cash for small expenses.

9. Be Weather Sensitive: Check weather conditions estimates and pack as needs be, particularly if you intend to participate in open-air exercises.

10. Nearby Occasions: Watch out for nearby celebrations and occasions during your visit. Partaking in Swiss customs can add social profundity to your outing.

11. Security First: Switzerland is by and large protected, however, it's wise to avoid potential risks like shielding your effects and complying with wellbeing rules for outside undertakings.

12. Investigate Locally: Find an opportunity to meander in Swiss towns and towns. You might find enchanting nearby shops, unexpected, yet invaluable treasures, and agreeable local people anxious to share their accounts.

13. Remain Adaptable: While arranging is fundamental, permit space for immediacy. Probably all those recollections can emerge out of startling revelations.

14. Catch Recollections: Bring a camera or cell phone to record your encounters and staggering Swiss views. Remember additional batteries or chargers.

15. Reach out to Locals: Draw in with Swiss individuals to acquire bits of knowledge into their way of life and way of life. Local people frequently have important suggestions for outside of what might be expected encounters.

16. Have Fun on the Way: Switzerland's scenes are stunning, so find an opportunity to see the value in the actual excursion, whether via train, streetcar or by walking.

Dining in Switzerland

Swiss cuisine combines international influences with hearty Alpine-inspired dishes in a delightful way. The following are essential components of Swiss cuisine:

1. Fondue: White wine, garlic, and melting cheese, typically a blend of Gruyère and Emmental, are the ingredients in this well-known Swiss dish. Using long forks, diners dip bread into the melting cheese. It's a common and comfortable eating experience.

2. Raclette: Raclette, like fondue, involves melting cheese, but it is typically served with boiled potatoes, pickles, and onions instead of dipping. The dissolved cheddar is scratched straightforwardly onto the plate.

3. Rösti: Frequently called the Swiss hash brown, rösti is a fresh potato dish that can be delighted in plain or with different garnishes like cheddar, bacon, or seared eggs. It's a good Swiss breakfast #1.

4. Zürcher Geschnetzeltes: This Zurich-inspired dish features sliced veal cooked in a mushroom-and-white wine sauce. Typically, it is accompanied by rösti.

5. Alplermagronen: Known as Swiss macaroni and cheddar, this consoling dish joins pasta, potatoes, cheddar, and onions, all heated flawlessly. It's exemplary in mountain locales.

6. Birchermüesli: This energizing breakfast dish was created by Swiss physician Maximilian Bircher-Brenner.

It consists of honey, grated apples, nuts, and rolled oats that have been soaked in yogurt or milk.

7. Swiss Chocolate: Swiss chocolate is well-known for its high quality. Swiss chocolatiers create a large number of pralines, truffles, and bars. Guests can enjoy chocolate tastings and even make their own chocolates.

8. Swiss Cheddar: Swiss cheddar assortments are well known around the world. Gruyère, Emmental, Appenzeller, and Tête de Moine are only a couple of models. Test them at nearby dairies or markets.

9. Swiss Sweets: Pastries like Engadin's Nusstorte (a nut tart) and the buttery Gipfeli (a croissant) can be found in Swiss patisseries.

10. Swiss liquor: The cantons of Valais, Vaud, and Ticino are primarily responsible for producing excellent wines in Switzerland. Attempt nearby assortments like Pinot Noir, Chasselas, and Merlot.

11. Sap of birch: Birch sap is a customary Swiss beverage. It is harvested from birch trees in the early spring and has a flavor that is mild and slightly sweet. It's an invigorating, occasional treat.

12. Culinary Occasions: Switzerland has different culinary occasions and celebrations. Try not to miss the Fête de l'Escalade in Geneva, highlighting chocolate cauldrons, or the Zibelemärit onion market in Bern.

13. Occasional Food: Seasonal changes influence Swiss cuisine. In the summer, enjoy lighter fare like salads and fresh berries; in the winter, rich stews, rosti, and hot chocolate are must-haves.

14. Swiss Lager: There is a growing craft beer scene in the nation. Drink Appenzeller, Calanda, or Quöllfrisch, three of the region's brews.

15. Swiss Herbals: Alpine herbs like alpenrose, juniper, and mountain thyme frequently contribute distinctive flavors to Swiss cuisine.

16. Swiss Breakfast: Begin your day with a conventional Swiss breakfast of bircher muesli, dry bread with Swiss cheddar, and fragrant espresso.

17. Local Strengths: Switzerland's different areas offer their culinary claims to fame. While traveling across the country, try some of the country's dishes.

18. Swiss Patisseries: Test Swiss cakes like Engadine nut cake and rich croissants at neighborhood bread shops.

Swiss food is a mouthwatering journey through the country's extensive culinary heritage. Swiss cuisine is sure to please your taste buds, whether you choose to savor traditional Alpine dishes or explore more contemporary interpretations. Good luck!

Eating Decorum

Switzerland, known for its rich culinary legacy, likewise has unmistakable eating customs and manners. To have a smooth dining experience in the country, familiarize yourself with these guidelines:

1. Making arrangements: It's prudent to reserve a spot, particularly at well-known eateries. The Swiss restaurant industry values punctuality.

2. Greeting: When entering a restaurant, Swiss diners typically exchange a cordial "Bonjour" or "Bonsoir" greeting. On leaving, a basic "Merci" (Thank you) is respectful.

3. Social graces: The manners of Swiss dining are typically European. keep your elbow and hands down from the tabl. Before you begin, you should wait for the host or hostess to start the meal or to say "Bon appétit."

4. Tipping: Administration charges are remembered for the bill, however, it's standard to gather together the aggregate or leave a little tip if help is extraordinary. 10% is an adequate tip for amazing assistance.

5. Water and Bread: Swiss eateries frequently serve water and bread, and these things might be charged. On the off chance that you don't need them, amiably decline when the server offers them.

6. Selection of Wine: Switzerland's wine selection is impressive. If all else fails, ask your server for wine suggestions to coordinate with your dinner.

7. Ordering: Trust that everybody at the table will be prepared before putting in your request. If the menu isn't in English, make sure to for an English menu.

8. Getting Paid: Typically, the bill is brought to your table; you don't have to request it. Installment is made at the counter. Mastercards are generally acknowledged.

9. Language: Switzerland has four authority dialects: German, French, Italian, and Romansh. Region by region, different languages are spoken. When possible, speak in the local language to the staff, but the majority speak English.

10. Level of Noise: The Swiss value a peaceful setting when dining. To keep the atmosphere calm, keep conversations at a moderate volume.

11. Dietary Inclinations: When you order, let your server know if you have any dietary restrictions, and they will do their best to meet your needs.

12. Children: Swiss cafés are for the most part youngster cordial. There are highchairs available, and children's menus frequently feature standard selections.

13. Punctuality: Make your reservations on time. Punctuality is important to Swiss diners.

14. Code of Dress: While easygoing clothing is adequate in numerous cafés, dressing somewhat more formally for upscale eating establishments is shrewd. Before you go, check the dress code of the restaurant.

15. Leftovers: Bringing extras back home from eateries is normal in Switzerland, and a team of servers will generally help with bundling.

16. Cell Phones: During meals, keep your phone on silent, and don't talk too loudly or take calls at the table.

17. Fondue with Cheese: While enjoying cheddar fondue, follow the nearby custom: try not to lose your bread in the cheddar, or you may be supposed to purchase drinks all around.

18. Coffee in the Carafe: Swiss custom directs that espresso is served after dessert, so don't be astounded if it's excluded from your dinner.

Options for Accommodation

Switzerland has a wide range of options for lodging to suit a variety of budgets and preferences. Here is an outline of the kinds of spots you can remain during your visit:

1. Hotels: Switzerland has a lot of hotels, from 5-star resorts with opulence to budget-friendly options. You'll track down notable global chains and enchanting store lodgings. Hotels are most abundant in major cities like Zurich, Geneva, and Lucerne.

2. B&B (Bed and Breakfast): B&Bs offer a more intimate and familiar setting. They are a great choice because they are frequently situated in picturesque rural settings.

3. Hostels: Hostels offer dorm-style rooms with shared facilities like bathrooms and kitchens, making them ideal for travelers on a budget. Numerous modern, clean, and well-equipped Swiss hostels exist. They are particularly well-liked by young travelers and backpackers.

4. Guesthouses: Guesthouses give a blend of lodging and B&B encounters. They offer comfortable, agreeable rooms and breakfast administration. Guesthouses are normal in rustic regions, giving a valid Swiss encounter.

5. Excursion Rentals: Apartments, chalets, and villas are just a few of the vacation rentals available in Switzerland. These are ideally suited for families or gatherings searching for additional space and self-cooking choices. There are numerous listings all over the country on platforms like Airbnb.

6. Alpine Cabins: For those looking for experience in the Swiss Alps, high cottages give fundamental convenience in staggering mountain areas. They are frequently utilized by explorers, climbers, and skiers and give a provincial encounter common dozing regions and shared offices.

7. Mountain Resorts: Swiss mountain resorts, like Zermatt, Verbier, and St. Moritz, offer upscale inns and chalets. They are prestigious for their elite skiing in the colder time of year and outside exercises in the late spring. High-end amenities and stunning views are to be expected.

8. Spa and wellness resorts: Switzerland is renowned for its well-being and spa resorts, especially in places like Terrible Ragaz and Baden. These lavish foundations center around unwinding, restoration, and warm showers.

9. Farm Remains Experience: Swiss rustic life by remaining on a functioning ranch. Guest accommodations and the opportunity to participate in daily farm activities are common on numerous farms. This choice is great for families and nature devotees.

10. Camping: Outdoor enthusiasts frequently choose to camp. Switzerland has very much kept up with camping areas in gorgeous regular settings. Electricity, showers, and communal kitchens are just a few of the many amenities available at campgrounds.

11. of kind Facilities: Igloos, treehouses, and even a hotel made entirely of ice are among the unusual lodging options available in Switzerland. These choices give vital stays to audacious explorers.

While picking your convenience, consider factors like area, spending plan, and the kind of involvement you need. Remember that Switzerland's high season, particularly in the Alps, can be occupied, so it's prudent to book facilities well ahead of time, particularly during top travel periods like summer and winter. Whether you favor the cosmopolitan appeal of urban areas or the serenity of mountain towns, Switzerland offers assorted and agreeable spots to rest during your visit.

Chapter 7: Navigating Swiss Transportation

Switzerland is famous for its productive and broad transportation organization, making it simple for voyagers to investigate the country's different scenes and attractions. A comprehensive guide to Swiss public transportation is provided below:

1. Trains: Swiss trains are popular for their reliability, tidiness, and solace. The Swiss Federal Railways (SBB) runs a vast network that connects cities, towns, and even inaccessible areas. The Glacier Express and Bernina Express are two scenic train routes that provide breathtaking views of the Alps. Consider buying a Swiss Travel Pass for limitless train travel during your visit.

2. Buses and trams: In Swiss urban communities, cable cars and transports are the essential methods of metropolitan transportation. The tram systems in Bern, Geneva, Basel, and Zurich are well-developed. Tickets can be bought at stations or through versatile applications, and they're frequently legitimate for cable cars, transports, and boats inside unambiguous zones.

3. Boats and Ships: There are numerous opportunities for scenic boat rides on Switzerland's lakes. Lake Geneva, Lake Lucerne, and Lake Zurich are famous decisions. Seeing Switzerland's natural beauty from the water is fun on boats and ferries.

4. Streetcars and Funiculars: Switzerland has numerous funicular railways and cable cars that connect high-altitude destinations and hiking areas because of its mountainous terrain. These are fundamental for investigating the Alps and appreciating winter sports.

5. Rental Vehicles: While Swiss public transportation is great, leasing a vehicle can be a helpful choice if you intend to investigate distant regions. However, before selecting a rental car, take into account the country's efficient train system, parking fees, and traffic regulations.

6. Travel Passes: Consider purchasing passes for unlimited travel within Switzerland, depending on your travel plans. Along with free or discounted admission to numerous museums and attractions, the Swiss Travel Pass covers trains, buses, trams, and boats.

7. Tickets and schedules: Swiss public transportation works on an exact timetable, so make certain to likewise really take a look at schedules and plan your excursions. Tickets can be bought at stations, on the web, or through versatile applications. Most train stations have ticket machines in numerous dialects.

8. Apps for Swiss Travel: Swiss Travel Framework offers a few supportive applications, for example, the SBB Versatile application for train timetables and tickets, and the SBB Review for live train following. For city travel, public transportation apps like ZVV in Zurich and TPG in Geneva are also helpful.

9. Services for bags: Swiss stations frequently give gear capacity and move administrations, making it helpful to investigate between registration and look at times. Label your bags with your destination at all times.

10. Rail Tickets: Switzerland offers different rail passes, including the Swiss Travel Pass, Swiss Half Toll Card, and provincial passes. If you plan to use trains frequently, these can save you a lot of money.

11. Go in Solace: Tickets for first-class travel provide additional comfort, quieter cabins, and more space. However, second-class tickets are extremely cost-effective and comfortable.

You'll have no trouble getting around Switzerland thanks to its scenic and effective transportation system. Swiss transportation will make your journey as memorable as the destination, whether you're looking out the window of a train in the Alps, floating on a tranquil lake, or taking a cable car up a mountain.

Tips for Safety and Well-Being

Switzerland is an Amazingly Safe and Well-Being Destination for Tourists. Nonetheless, it's consistently shrewd to be ready and informed to guarantee a smooth and pleasant excursion. Here are fundamental wellbeing and wellbeing tips for your visit:

1. Safety

a. Low Rate of Crime: Switzerland is a safe destination for tourists because it has one of the lowest rates of crime in the world. Still, take common sense precautions like keeping your belongings safe and being careful in crowded areas.

b. Help in an emergency: Switzerland has a solid crisis reaction framework. For general emergencies, dial 112 or 117 for the police.

c. Threats from Nature: Switzerland is inclined to normal dangers like torrential slides in the colder time of year and periodic floods. When planning activities in the mountains, check the weather and safety conditions.

D. Mountain Security: Be well-prepared with the appropriate gear, maps, and terrain knowledge if you plan to hike or ski in the Alps. Regard trail markings and follow any alerts or terminations.

e. Safety in Water: The lakes in Switzerland are tempting, but always adhere to safety precautions when swimming or participating in water sports. Follow the lifeguard's instructions and pay attention to warning signs.

2. Health

a. Health care coverage: Guarantee you have exhaustive travel protection that covers health-related crises and bringing home. Healthcare in Switzerland is of the highest quality, but it can be pricey for tourists.

b. Immunizations: In most cases, vaccinations are not necessary to enter Switzerland. Nonetheless, counsel your primary care physician in regards to routine immunizations and any extra suggestions.

c. Height Disorder: Be aware of altitude sickness symptoms like headaches and nausea if you plan to visit high-altitude areas like the Swiss Alps and acclimate gradually.

d. Water: Regular water is protected to drink all through Switzerland. Convey a reusable water jug to lessen plastic waste.

e. Safety of Food: Swiss food is by and large protected. Practice standard food cleanliness, and be wary of unpasteurized dairy items and half-cooked meat.

f. Sunscreening: Use sunscreen, wear sunglasses, and shield yourself from the sun when you're outside to avoid getting burned.

3. Coronavirus Contemplations

a. Requirements: Switzerland has carried out Coronavirus wellbeing measures, including veil orders and inoculation prerequisites for certain exercises. Take a look at neighborhood guidelines and rules previously and during your outing.

b. Immunization and Testing: Confirm Switzerland's entrance prerequisites in regards to immunization or testing, as they might change. Keep your immunization card and experimental outcomes convenient.

c. Travel Limitations: Remain refreshed on movement limitations and passage necessities for Switzerland, as they might differ given your nation of origin.

d. Hygiene and Health: Practice physical distancing and wearing masks in indoor public spaces, among other recommended health and hygiene practices.

e. Coronavirus Testing: Find out more about testing areas and systems in Switzerland on the off chance that you want to get tried during your excursion.

Switzerland's obligation to somewhere safe and secure and superb medical services guidelines guarantees a protected and effortless travel insight. You'll be well-prepared to take in everything this stunning nation has to offer if you follow these health and safety guidelines.

Emergency Contacts

To ensure your safety and well-being while traveling in Switzerland, it is essential to know your emergency contact information. The following are essential emergency contacts:

1. Services for General Emergencies

- Crisis Administrations: For general emergencies, dial 112.
- Police: For police assistance, dial 117.

2. Assistance with Medicine

- Emergency vehicle/Paramedics: For medical emergencies, including illnesses and accidents, dial 144.

3. Department of Fire

- Fire and Salvage: Dial 118 to report fires or other related crises.

4. Emergency aides

- The Swiss Automobile Club Dial 140 for vehicle breakdown help.

5. Consular Help

- On the off chance that you are a far-off public needing help from your international haven or department, contact the important discretionary mission. The official websites of embassies and consulates typically contain contact information.

6. Mountain Aid

- In uneven areas, particularly the Swiss Alps, if you require salvage or help during open-air exercises, for example, climbing or skiing, contact the neighborhood mountain salvage administration.
- Rega (Swiss Air Salvage): For air ambulance and mountain rescue services, dial 1414.

7. Poison Control Center

Toxicological Data Community: For poison-related emergencies, dial 145.

8. Lost or Taken Visas

- Contact your Mastercard supplier quickly to report lost or taken cards. The contact number can commonly be found on the rear of the card or the card guarantor's site.

9. The travel industry Hotline

- On the off chance that you have non-crisis questions or require vacationer data, you can call the Switzerland travel industry Hotline.
- Switzerland Travel Assistance: For inquiries from tourists, dial 00800 100 200 29.

It's fitting to save these crisis numbers in your telephone or keep them in a promptly open area while going to Switzerland. In the event of any unforeseen circumstances, Switzerland's effective emergency response system ensures that assistance is readily available.

Travel Protection

Travel protection is a fundamental part of arranging an excursion to Switzerland. It gives monetary assurance and true serenity if there should be an occurrence of unforeseen occasions during your excursion. What you need to know about Swiss travel insurance is as follows:

1. Kinds of Movement Protection

- **Clinical service:** This covers clinical costs, including specialist visits, hospitalization, and crisis clinical clearing.
- **Trip Delay or Cancellation:** reimburses non-refundable trip costs if you have to cancel or shorten your trip for covered reasons, protecting your investment.
- **Personal Property and Baggage:** covers personal items and luggage that are damaged, lost, or stolen.

- **Travel Deferral:** Repays extra costs caused because of surprising travel delays.
- **Help in an Emergency:** provides 24/7 emergency assistance for situations such as medical evacuations.
- **Coverage of Adventure Sports:** On the off chance that you intend to take part in experience exercises, guarantee your strategy covers them.

2. Significance of Movement Protection

- Clinical consideration in Switzerland can be costly for explorers, so clinical service is essential.
- Safeguards against monetary misfortunes brought about by trip scratch-offs, interferences, or postponements.
- Offers inward feeling of harmony, particularly while going during eccentric times, like the Coronavirus pandemic.

3. Purchasing Travel Protection

- You can buy travel protection through protection suppliers, travel services, or online stages.
- Read the policy carefully to learn what is covered and what is not.
- Consider factors like your well-being, trip span, arranged exercises, and the worth of your effects while picking inclusion.

4. European Health Care Coverage Card (EHIC)

- Carry your EHIC, which grants you access to necessary Swiss medical care if you are a citizen of the EU or EFTA. In any case, it's anything but a substitute for movement protection as it may not cover all costs.

5. Coronavirus Inclusion

- Check if your movement protection covers coronavirus-related costs, like testing, treatment, and quarantine costs.

- COVID-19 cancellation and interruption coverage is provided by some policies.

6. Claims Cycle

- Keep duplicates of all receipts, clinical records, and episode reports on the off chance that you want to make a case.
- In the event of an emergency, get in touch with your insurance provider as soon as possible.

7. Protection Suppliers

- Consider trustworthy insurance agencies like Allianz, Travel Watchman, and World Migrants, or contrast arrangements through internet-based stages to track down the best inclusion for your necessities.

8. Crisis Contacts

- Keep a physical copy of your policy documents on you and save the emergency contact number for your insurance provider in your phone.

9. Span of Inclusion

- Check to see that your travel insurance covers the entire trip. Having satisfactory travel protection is an insightful speculation while visiting Switzerland. It guarantees you're monetarily safeguarded in unexpected conditions and can completely partake in your Swiss experience with genuine serenity.

Chapter 8: Packing Tips and Travel Checklist

Pressing for your Switzerland experience requires cautious thought to guarantee you're good to go for shifting atmospheric conditions, open-air exercises, and social investigation. Here is a complete pressing aid and travel agenda to assist you with pressing productively:

1. Important Documents

- Identification with something like a half-year's legitimacy
- Visa (whenever required)
- Copies of significant records (put away independently)

2. Travel protection records

- Power connector and voltage converter if necessary (Switzerland utilizes Type J plugs)
- Various credit/charge cards and a few Swiss Francs in real money

- Compact charger and travel connectors for gadgets

3. Clothing

Due to the varying weather, layers are essential. Pack lightweight, dampness-wicking base layers, warm layers, and a waterproof, breathable coat.

- Sweaters or wools for warmth
- Agreeable, dampness-wicking climbing pants or open-air pants
- Open to strolling shoes with great footing for investigating towns and trails
- Additional socks, including a fleece or warm socks for outside exercises
- Warm cap, gloves, and a scarf
- Swimwear for lakes and warm showers
- Agreeable sleepwear

4. Toiletries and Individual Consideration

A clear, resealable bag containing travel-sized toiletries, sunscreen, lip balm, insect repellent, and a basic first-aid kit with bandages, pain relievers, and other items

- Doctor-prescribed drugs and duplicates of medicines
- Individual cleanliness things

5. Outside Stuff (If Pertinent)

- Climbing boots or shoes
- Daypack for climbing with basics like water, snacks, and a guide
- Journeying posts whenever wanted
- Optics for untamed life and picturesque survey

6. Electronics

Chargers and cables, as well as a portable power bank and a universal plug adapter for smartphones, tablets, and laptops. Travel Solace:

- Neck cushion for long flights or train rides

- Eye veil and earplugs for better rest
- Lightweight, reduced umbrella or downpour raincoat
- Reusable water bottle

8. Travel Guides and Guides

- Printed travel guides or guides (or download computerized renditions)
- Swiss Rail Pass or transportation passes if pertinent

9. Language

A Swiss-German, French, Italian, or Romansh phrasebook or app (if you don't know the local languages) Entertainment:

- Books, tablets, or book recordings for free time
- Downloaded motion pictures or shows for disconnected survey

11. **Miscellaneous**

- Reusable shopping sacks for eco-accommodating shopping
- Ziplock sacks for putting away bites or wet things
- Travel clothing cleanser bundles (for longer excursions)

Travel sewing pack

Before takeoff, actually look at your movement agenda to guarantee you haven't failed to remember any basics. With the right planning, you'll be prepared to investigate Switzerland's shocking scenes, enjoy nearby food, and make remarkable recollections during your Swiss experience. Safe voyages!

Valuable Expressions and Language Guide

Switzerland is a multilingual country with four authority dialects: German, French, Italian, and Romansh. Although many Swiss people speak English, it is always appreciated when tourists attempt to communicate in their native tongue. Here are a few valuable expressions and language tips for every one of the significant locales:

German-Speaking Switzerland (Schweizerdeutsch)

1. Hello - Hallo

2. Good morning - Guten Morgen

3. Good afternoon - Guten Tag

4. Good evening - Guten Abend

5. Goodbye - Auf Wiedersehen

6. Please - Bitte

7. Thank you - Danke

8. Yes - Ja

9. No - Nein

10. Excuse me / Sorry - Entschuldigung

11. I don't understand - Ich verstehe nicht

12. How much does this cost? - Wie viel kostet das?

13. Where is the restroom? - Wo ist die Toilette?

14. I need help - Ich brauche Hilfe

15. I'm lost - Ich habe mich verirrt

16. Do you speak English? - Sprechen Sie Englisch?

French-Speaking Switzerland (Suisse romande)

1. Hello - Bonjour

2. Good morning - Bonjour (used throughout the day)

3. Good afternoon - Bon après-midi

4. Good evening - Bonsoir

5. Goodbye - Au revoir

6. Please - S'il vous plaît

7. Thank you - Merci

8. Yes - Oui

9. No - Non

10. Excuse me / Sorry - Excusez-moi

11. I don't understand - Je ne comprends pas

12. How much does this cost? - Combien ça coûte?

13. Where is the restroom? - Où sont les toilettes?

14. I need help - J'ai besoin d'aide

15. I'm lost - Je suis perdu(e)

16. Do you speak English? - Parlez-vous anglais?

Italian-Speaking Switzerland (Svizzera italiana)

1. Hello - Ciao / Buongiorno

2. Good morning - Buongiorno

3. Good afternoon - Buon pomeriggio

4. Good evening - Buonasera

5. Goodbye - Arrivederci

6. Please - Per favore

7. Thank you - Grazie

8. Yes - Sì

9. No - No

10. Excuse me / Sorry - Scusate / Mi dispiace

11. I don't understand - Non capisco

12. How much does this cost? - Quanto costa?

13. Where is the restroom? - Dov'è il bagno?

14. I need help - Ho bisogno di aiuto

15. I'm lost - Mi sono perso(a)

16. Do you speak English? - Parlate inglese?

Romansh-Speaking Switzerland

Romansh is the least spoken of Switzerland's official languages, primarily found in the canton of Graubünden. Here are some basic phrases:

1. Hello - Allegra

2. Good morning - Bun di

3. Goodbye - Ciau

4. Thank you - Grazia fitg

5. Yes - Tgi

6. No - Betg

7. I don't understand - Jeu na chapesch betg

8. Do you speak English? - Vus parles englais?

You can enhance your travel experience and demonstrate respect for the local culture by learning a few phrases in the language. Most Swiss individuals value any work you make to impart in their language, regardless of whether it's a hello or a basic "much obliged."

Printed in Great Britain
by Amazon